Lancashire Recipes

A selection of Recipes from around Lancashire

By **Linzi Barrow**

BRADWELL
BOOKS

Published by Bradwell Books

9 Orgreave Close Sheffield S13 9NP

Email: books@bradwellbooks.co.uk

British Library Cataloguing in Publication Data: a catalogue record for this book is available from the British Library.

1st Edition

ISBN: 9781902674438

Print: Cambrian Printers Aberystwyth SY23 3TN

Design by: Andrew Caffrey

Edited by: Louise Maskill

Photographic Credits:
  Joan Ransley, Hugh Marrows & ShutterStock

Front Cover:
  Left - right: Lamb casserole, Travellight/Shutterstock; Parkin, Monkey Business Images/Shutterstock
  Poached egg and asparagus, Fotogroove/Shutterstock; Verkhovynets Taras/Shutterstock
  Bottom, George Green/Shutterstock

Back Page:
  Kevin Eaves/Shutterstock

Title Page:
  Lancashire Hot Pot, Monkey Business Images/Shutterstock

The photographs used in this book are to illustrate the dish and are not meant as a final representation of the finished result. Any garnish or additions are at your discretion.

Contents

Introduction

George Green/Shutterstock

Lancashire is a county with a proud culinary heritage. Its geography firmly influences the produce and the dishes that call this county home.

The county is fortunate to have hills and moorland which produce superb lamb and game, quality grazing land which enables the raising of high quality beef and dairy herds, and low-lying mosslands which are home to fantastic vegetable and fruit growers.

Luckily for us its coastline also enables a wide range of fish and shellfish to be available in the region. A humble honest northern cuisine has evolved in the county, utilising the great local produce with a frugal approach to ingredients and the emphasis on taste rather than looks.

Lancashire, land of the hotpot, the county where beef became sirloin, is now home to a thriving high-quality food scene where one can eat very well. The county's produce is now valued nationally and internationally, some its famous exports being Lancashire cheese, Morecambe bay shrimps and Goosnargh poultry.

Essentially that's where I come in. I am the author of a popular food blog Lancashire Food, which initially started as a vehicle to share my love of the county's great dishes and fabulous ingredients. However, it has recently grown and become so much more. My own Lancashire culinary heritage is of being taught to cook by my Nanna and my Mum, but other than domestic science lessons at school I have no formal training; I am a home cook, I love baking and creating recipes and also eating out, and I feel that being able to cook with high quality produce is a right not a privilege. That's why I was delighted to be invited to compile a modern Lancashire recipe book.

Kevin Eaves/Shutterstock

Lancashire Oatcak

These are a little-known delicacy from the county, very similar to the Staffordshire oatcake but difficult to find in the shops, so I have resorted to making my own. I have fond childhood memories of having these spread with butter and jam as a teatime treat after a shopping trip in Preston; my father particularly enjoyed them spread with treacle. They can also be left to harden and they may then be served to accompany stews.

Ingredients

450g fine ground oatmeal

2 tsp dried yeast

2 tsp sea salt

1 dsp vegetable oil

1.5 l hand-hot water

Method

1   Mix all the ingredients in a large bowl until you have a smooth batter. Leave to ferment for approximately 1 hour in a warm place.

2   When the mixture is bubbly you are ready to griddle the oatcakes. Heat a heavy based frying pan or a griddle plate, lubricate with a little vegetable oil and remove the excess with a piece of kitchen towel; the oatcakes are best if they are dry-fried.

3   Pour a large ladleful of the mixture into the pan. It will spread to make a large pancake-like shape. Cook gently until small bubbles can be seen on the surface and the surface is drying out.

4   Turn and cook briefly on the other side. Allow to cool on a clean tea towel while you cook the rest of the mixture.

Jamie Rogers/ShutterStock

Soda Bread

There are many artisan bakers around Lancashire, but there is nothing quite like filling the house with the smell of home-baked bread. It is much easier than most people think, especially using the sodabread recipe below; you'll get one largish loaf or three smaller ones. Soda bread tends to be denser than yeasted bread, so don't be surprised if it doesn't rise quite as much as you might expect.

Ingredients

400g wholemeal flour

75g plain white flour (you can use strong bread flour if you have it)

1 tsp salt

1 tsp bicarbonate of soda

1 large egg

1 tbsp vegetable oil of your choice

1 tsp honey, treacle or soft brown sugar, whichever you have to hand

425ml buttermilk or sour milk*

*To make sour milk, take 425ml milk, add the juice of ½ a lemon, give it a quick stir, leave for 10 minutes and off you go.

Method

1. Preheat the oven to 200oC, gas 6. Prepare a loaf tin (23 x 12.5 x 5cm) by brushing with vegetable oil or lining with a paper liner, or use smaller tins if you prefer.

2. Put the dry ingredients into a large bowl and sieve in the bicarbonate of soda. Mix well.

3. Whisk the egg and then add the oil, sugar/honey/treacle and the buttermilk or sour milk. Make a well in the centre of the dry ingredients and pour in all the liquid. Using a large wooden spoon mix well, scraping the flour from the sides until all the ingredients are blended into a smooth, slightly gloopy mixture. Add more milk if necessary.

4. Pour into the loaf tin(s) and sprinkle on some seeds on top if you fancy (sunflower seeds or linseeds are nice).

5. Put in the oven for an hour and then check to see if the loaf is cooked through using a skewer. If the bread is ready it will sound hollow when you knock it on the bottom, and the skewer should come out clean.

Space Monkey Pics/ShutterStock

Basic Stock

A good stock is the basis for many soups, stews, casseroles and pie fillings. Of course, there are lots of different methods for making instant stock, and there's no shame in that, but here is an easy way of making your own and storing it for later use.

Ingredients

1.75l water

A handful of fresh white button mushrooms, sliced

1 large onion, chopped

1 large leek, chopped

1 large carrot, chopped

1 celery stick, including the leafy top, sliced

Method

1   Place the vegetables in the water and bring to the boil. Simmer for 45 minutes.

2   Pass through a strainer lined with muslin, and then use or store. Stock will keep in a covered container in the fridge for up to four days, or store it in small quantities in the freezer for later use.

3   For fish stock, boil 1.5kg fish bones, including the heads, in the water for 20 minutes before adding the vegetables.

4   For beef stock, bake 1kg of beef bones (available from your butcher) in the oven until well browned. Add them to the water with the vegetables and simmer for a bit longer – up to two hours.

5   For chicken stock, use the bones from a cooked chicken carcass, including the skin. Simmer for up to two hours.

6   You can also season according to your own taste – garlic can be added with the vegetables, a few peppercorns add a depth of flavour, and bay leaves or even a bouquet garni may be used.

Omelette

A good omelette is one of the most basic dishes in any cook's repertoire, but it is almost endlessly versatile. Dress it up with cheese (Lancashire, of course, but Cheddar and Parmesan are also good), mushrooms, ham, bacon, herbs, leftover vegetables – whatever you have to hand.

Ingredients

2 large or **3** medium eggs

2 knobs of butter

Salt and pepper

Monkey Business Images/Shutterstock

Method

1   Warm a non-stick frying pan on a medium heat. Crack the eggs into a bowl and beat them with a fork so they break up and mix, but not as completely as you would for scrambled egg.

2   With the heat on medium-hot, drop one knob of butter into the pan. Season the eggs with a little salt and pepper, and pour into the pan. Let the eggs bubble slightly for a couple of seconds, then take a wooden fork or spatula and gently draw the mixture in from the sides of the pan a few times, so it gathers in folds in the centre.

3   Leave for a few seconds, then stir again to lightly combine uncooked egg with cooked. Leave briefly again, and when partly cooked, stir a bit faster, stopping while there's some barely cooked egg left.

4   With the pan flat on the heat, shake it back and forth a few times to settle the mixture. It should slide easily in the pan and look soft and moist on top. A quick burst of heat will brown the underside.

5   Tilt the pan away from you and fold the side of omelette nearest to you over on top of the lower half. Slide onto a warmed plate and serve immediately.

6   To dress up your omelette, add finely grated cheese to the beaten eggs before you put the mixture in the pan, or add other ingredients half way through the cooking time, when you are stirring the omelette to combine cooked and uncooked egg.

Simple Tomato Sa

A good tomato sauce is the foundation for so many wonderful dishes – pizza, pasta, chicken, casseroles, fish... Here is a recipe for a basic tomato sauce. It is simple and delicious by itself, but it can be dressed up with mushrooms, sausage, olives, wine, and all manner of vegetables. Don't worry if you haven't got the fresh herbs listed below; dried will do just as well (use half the quantity given below), or mix and match to your own taste.

Ingredients

2 tbsp olive oil

½ medium onion, finely chopped

1 small carrot or ½ large carrot, finely chopped

1 small stalk of celery, including the green tops, finely chopped

2 tbsp fresh parsley, chopped

1 clove garlic, crushed

2 tbsp fresh basil, chopped

1 400g tin chopped tomatoes, including the juice

1 tsp tomato puree

Salt and freshly ground black pepper to taste

Method

1   Heat the olive oil in a large wide-based pan on a medium heat. Add the chopped onion, carrot, celery and parsley. Stir to coat in the oil.

2   Reduce the heat to low, cover the pan and cook for 15 to 20 minutes, stirring occasionally until the vegetables are softened and cooked through.

3   Remove the cover and add the crushed garlic. Increase the heat to medium high. Cook the garlic for a few seconds. Add the tomatoes, including the juice, the tomato puree and the basil. Season with salt and pepper to taste.

4   Bring to a low simmer, reduce the heat to low and cook uncovered until the sauce is thickened (about 15 minutes). If you want to give the sauce a smooth consistency you could blend it.

5   Store in the fridge, or freeze until needed.

Galina Gutarin/Shutterstock

Courgette Soup

In the summertime we are always overrun with courgettes from the garden, and this recipe came about to use up lots of them! However, when they are in season courgettes are inexpensive to purchase for this easy soup which freezes well. If you fancy playing with the colour of the soup you could use yellow or gold courgettes instead.

Ingredients

4 or **5** medium sized courgettes, cut into slices

1 large onion, peeled and finely chopped

Olive oil or butter

A couple of bay leaves

500ml good quality vegetable stock (you could make your own, but powder or a cube is fine)

Salt and pepper

Method

1   Melt the butter in a large saucepan or preheat your oil. Add the onion and
    cook gently over a low heat without colouring until softened slightly.

2   Add the courgettes and cook until slightly softened. Now add the vegetable
    stock and the bay leaves. Bring to the boil and then reduce the heat and
    simmer until all the vegetables
    are soft.

3   Remove the bay leaves. Blitz
    with a hand blender or use a
    liquidizer or food processor to
    blitz until smooth.

4   Reheat and taste for seasoning,
    adding salt and pepper to taste.
    Serve with bread (perhaps the
    sodabread from earlier in this
    book), and you could also top
    grated with Parmesan cheese
    if you like.

Travellight/Shutterstock

Fish Parcels

The coastal area of Lancashire is generally flat and sandy, and is more famous for its treacherous tides and sinking sand that for its glorious beaches. Therefore, most of the fish caught locally is of the flat variety, or the type that swim in tidal estuaries.

However, the town of Fleetwood is famous for deep-sea fishing. In the industry's heyday tons of cod, haddock and other fish were landed at the port, although now it is a shadow of its former self. This recipe works with most fish, although I like it with salmon.

Ingredients

1 fillet of fish per portion (you could use salmon, cod, pollack etc.)

A couple of lemon slices (optional)

Fish stock (see the recipe earlier in this book)

Fresh herbs (you get a better result with fresh, but you can use always use dried instead)

Baking parchment or aluminium foil

Salt and pepper

Lancashire cheese, grated

Method

1. Pre-heat your oven to 180C/gas 4. Prepare pieces of foil or baking parchment big to make a reasonable sized parcel for each fillet of fish.

2. Place the fish in the middle of the foil or parchment and form up the sides of the parcel. If using lemon slices, place them under the fish fillet. Sprinkle with a little fish stock, seasoning and some herbs.

3. Close up your parcel, being careful not to lose your stock. Place in the pre-heated oven on a baking tray. Bake for around 10 minutes; the exact cooking time will depend on the fish and its thickness.

4. When the fish is cooked, remove from the parcel, sprinkle with a handful of grated Lancashire cheese and grill until melted and golden. Serve with a salad garnish as a starter, or accompanied by salad and boiled new potatoes as a main course.

Christopher Elwell/Shutterstock

Tomato Soup

The mossland areas of Lancashire have been a centre of market gardening for many years. The rich black soil grows fabulous salads and vegetables, and the area around Tarleton is famous for its tomatoes, so here is a recipe inspired by the flavourful tomatoes that are grown in the area. Out of season you can use imported varieties if you need to, but I find tinned or even frozen homegrown tomatoes give a better-tasting result. I also don't go in for skinning the tomatoes; I prefer to sieve the soup to remove the pips and skin. This would also be an opportunity to use the stock recipe earlier in this book!

Ingredients

1 kilo tomatoes, chopped into chunky pieces

1 large onion, chopped finely

Vegetable stock

Pinch of sugar

Salt and pepper

An optional herb of your choice (basil, rosemary, thyme or tarragon work well)

Small amount of cornflour to thicken

Small knob of butter or vegetable oil

Method

1	Take a large pan and melt the butter. Add the onion first and cook until softened slightly, but without colouring.
2	Add the chopped tomatoes to the pan and cook until they start to soften. Now add your chosen herb, if using, and enough vegetable stock to cover. Add a pinch of sugar and simmer until all the vegetables are very soft.
3	Sieve the soup back into the rinsed pan to remove skins, pips and stalks, rubbing through with a wooden spoon. Bring the soup back up to a gentle simmer and add the cornflour mixed to a paste with a little water to thicken the soup.
4	Taste for seasoning and add salt and pepper to taste. Serve with chunky slices of homemade bread (perhaps made using the soda bread recipe earlier in this book).

Bjonesphotography/Shutterstock

Lancashire Chees

Lancashire cheese is creamy and delicious, and goes beautifully with the zingy flavours of this salad.

Ingredients

Bunch of mint

Small punnet of Lancashire tomatoes, sliced

Half a red onion, sliced

Zest and juice of a lemon

2 tbsp olive oil

Good handful of crumbled up Lancashire cheese

e Salad

Method

1 Put the sliced tomatoes on a big plate. Tear the mint leaves and scatter over the tomatoes.

2 Sprinkle the slices of red onion on top along with the zest of the lemon. Mix the juice of the lemon with the olive oil and drizzle over the top.

3 Add the crumbled cheese and toss all the ingredients together. Serve as a starter to share with bread, or as an accompaniment to a main course.

Melica/Shutterstock

Tomato and Lanc Cheese Risotto

Another recipe using Lancashire's signature cheese, along with locally-grown tomatoes if you can get them. This risotto would work equally well served in small portions as an elegant starter, perhaps with a salad garnish, or as a comforting supper dish. This would be another opportunity to use the recipe for home-made stock earlier in this book.

Ingredients

250g Arborio rice

500ml chicken or vegetable stock (hot)

Generous knob of butter

1 large shallot, finely chopped

1 clove garlic, finely grated

2 large Lancashire tomatoes, chopped

100ml white wine

150g creamy Lancashire cheese

Sea salt

Freshly ground black pepper

Method

1   Melt the butter in a deep pan. Add the shallot and garlic and sweat until soft but not brown. Add the rice and stir until all the grains are coated in the butter. Season, add the wine and simmer until the wine has evaporated.

2   Add the stock a ladle-full at a time; do not add any more until the rice has absorbed the last ladle-full. Keep stirring the rice gently.

3   After cooking the rice for about ten minutes with additions of stock, add the chopped tomatoes. Keep stirring and continue to add the stock as before until the rice is al dente.

4   Crumble the Lancashire cheese into the rice and fold in so that the cheese melts. Check seasoning and add salt and pepper to taste.

5   Cover, remove from the heat and rest for five minutes. Serve in small ramekins with chopped tomato pieces and a basil garnish for a starter, or with hunks of bread as a comforting supper dish.

Tarasyuk Igor/Shutterstock   de2marco/Shutterstock

Lamb Casserole

This casserole is a favourite in our household, an easy dish ideal for the weekend especially when served with hunks of your favourite bread. It is a very forgiving recipe, because you can use whatever vegetables you have in the cupboard. The casserole is bulked up using beans, which have a natural affinity with lamb. I use meat sourced from a local farm; it's much better quality than the supermarket, and a good deal cheaper too. Why not ask your butcher about purchasing some local lamb?

Ingredients

Casserole lamb – a suitable quantity for the number of people you are serving, cut in to pieces

1 large white onion, peeled and chopped into chunks

fresh thyme, a small bunch

2 garlic cloves, peeled and finely chopped

1 tin butter beans or cannellini beans, drained and rinsed

1 tin plum tomatoes

lamb stock – from a cube or powder, unless you have made your own

A squirt of tomato puree

2 sticks of celery, chopped

2 large carrots, peeled and chopped

1 can of mild or stout

Additional vegetables – you could use swede or parsnip (optional)

1 tbsp flour, seasoned with salt and pepper

a little oil

Method

1   Pre-heat the oven to 160C/gas 3. Toss the lamb in the seasoned flour;
    I use a plastic bag to make things easy and less messy.

2   Heat a little oil in a pan and brown the lamb in batches. Don't crowd the pan,
    you are aiming to colour, not sweat. Remove to a casserole dish. In the same
    pan, fry the onion, carrot, celery and garlic. Remove these to the casserole
    dish too.

3   Deglaze the pan using the tin of tomatoes and the can of mild or stout. Bring
    to a simmer and then pour into your casserole dish. Add the thyme, the
    tomato puree and the extra vegetable if you're using them, stir to mix the
    meat and vegetables and put the lid on the casserole.

4   Place the casserole dish in the oven and cook for 2 hours. Give it casserole
    a good stir and add the drained beans. Cook until the casserole is thickened
    and the lamb very tender.

5   Serve with extra green vegetables and bread or potatoes.

Travellight/Shutterstock

Sausage Bake

Every summer we make this bake for our barbeque party. It's a popular dish which uses produce from the garden yet is teamed with that family favourite – sausages. I buy my sausages from the local butcher, and I suggest you do the same so that you can ask questions what has gone into them. Herby or tomato sausages work well in this recipe, but I have used spicy ones in the past and they were also delicious. It is also a great standby dish for a garden party (in case it rains!), and can even be cooked on top of the barbeque if you use a cast iron casserole.

Ingredients

6 thick sausages (whatever variety you want), chopped into bite-sized chunks

2 large white onions, peeled and roughly chopped

2 peppers (green or red), topped, de-seeded and roughly chopped

2 large courgettes, topped, tailed and roughly chopped

2 tins tomatoes or **1 kg** fresh tomatoes

2 garlic cloves

Fresh herbs – thyme, rosemary, basil
(or whatever you have in the garden or can get hold of)

Vegetable stock

Freshly ground black pepper

Method

1   I use a cast iron casserole (to save washing up), but if you don't have one then a frying pan and casserole dish can be used.

2   First, fry off the sausage pieces until they have taken some colour and lost some of the fat in them. You are going to use this fat to start off your vegetables. Remove the sausages from the pan to a plate.

3   Now fry the onion, garlic, peppers and courgettes until they have a little colour and are starting to soften. Add your tomatoes and fresh herbs and bring to a simmer.

4   Place the vegetable mixture and sausages together in the casserole dish. Depending on how much liquid is in your vegetables you may need to add a little vegetable stock.

5   Bake uncovered in the oven or on the hob or barbeque until everything is cooked and the stock reduced and thickened.

6   Serve with jacket potatoes, fresh bread or even rice or pasta

Travellight/Shutterstock

Vegetable Casse
Herb Dumplings

I have a couple of friends who are vegetarian, so I came up with this dish to enable all of us to share a lovely warming casserole on a winter's day. Although it contains no meat it will easily satisfy the most picky of meat eaters. It's also a pretty frugal dish as it just contains loads of seasonal vegetables. Personally I think the dumplings are essential, but you could omit them and serve with bread or potatoes instead.

Ingredients

2 or **3** large carrots, peeled and roughly chopped

2 or **3** parsnips, peeled, cored if very large and roughly chopped

1 large red onion, peeled and cut into eighths

2 med leeks roughly chopped

Approx 150g chestnut mushrooms (you can use white if you prefer)

2 cloves garlic, peeled and finely chopped

1 small butternut squash, peeled, de-seeded and roughly chopped

1 small swede, turnip or celeriac (all optional), peeled and roughly chopped

Olive oil

Dried wild mushrooms (soaked in water for about 15 minutes)

1 tbsp flour or cornflour, for thickening

Salt and pepper

For the dumplings

50g vegetable suet

100g self raising flour

Mixed dried herbs

Water

ole with

Method

1   Pre-heat the oven to 180C/gas 4.

2   Place the onion, carrots, parsnips, butternut squash and garlic in a roasting tray and toss them with a little olive oil. Roast for 20 to 30 minutes until the vegetables are slightly softened and golden in colour. Place them in your casserole dish.

3   Now cook the mushrooms in a little oil until softened. Add these to the casserole dish with the vegetables, add the flour and cook for a few minutes. Pour in enough vegetable stock to just cover the vegetables, give it a good stir, cover and place in the oven. Turn the oven temperature down to 160/gas 3.

4   Bake for around an hour, until the vegetables are tender and the sauce thickened slightly. Add more liquid if you need to.

For the dumplings

1   Mix the suet, flour and herbs and add enough water to bring it all together in a soft sticky dough. Using a little flour on your hands, form small balls of dough, plop them on the top of the casserole, replace the lid and bake for about 15 minutes more until the dumplings are soft and fluffy.

2   Serve immediately accompanied with a green vegetable if you like.

Ben Smith/Shutterstock

31

Grandad's Potato

Both my husband and I have fond memories of this dish from our childhood; it was a dish our grandparents would make when we were visiting. Given the frugality of the ingredients I would think it has its origins in the Second World War, as a useful vehicle to stretch out meagre rations to produce a dish which would feed a family. The dish requires no great cooking skills, just time and patience while it is in the oven. The resultant dish is a family favourite throughout Lancashire.

Ingredients

1 large old potato per person, peeled and sliced thinly

1 large white onion

Pinch dried thyme – or use fresh if you have it

1 rasher smoked bacon per person, chopped up into small pieces

Carrots, peeled and finely chopped (optional)

Vegetable or chicken stock (from a cube is fine)

Salt and pepper

Vegetable oil

Bake

Method

1   Pre-heat the oven to 160C/gas 3.

2   Dry-fry your bacon pieces in a frying pan until lightly golden. Remove from the pan and place on a plate.

3   In the same frying pan, soften the onions without colouring. The bacon fat should be enough to cook the onions, but add a little vegetable oil if you need to.

4   In your casserole dish, layer the potato slices, bacon pieces, onions and thyme (and the carrots if using), sprinkling each layer with a little salt and pepper (watch the level of salt because your bacon may already be quite salty).

5   Once you have layered your ingredients in the casserole dish, pour over enough stock to just cover everything. Place the lid on your casserole dish (or cover with foil if you don't have a lid), and place in the pre-heated oven.

6   Bake for approximately 2 hours, until the potatoes are soft and most of the stock has been absorbed. Remove the lid and bake for a further 30 to 50 minutes until the last of the stock has evaporated and the top is lightly golden and slightly crispy.

7   Serve accompanied by a green vegetable such as cabbage.

Jon Le-Bon/Shutterstock

Lancashire Hotpot

The iconic Lancashire dish, famous nationally and internationally. This is a true taste of home for any Lancastrian. In recent years chefs have started to re-invent this dish, but I don't think you can beat the true home-style version.

A debate rages as to whether the dish should include carrots or not. Here is my quick and easy version, which doesn't take too much effort to prepare and is great for all the family because it doesn't contain bones. I like to use a slow cooker for my hotpot, but if you don't have one a conventional oven will work fine too.

Ingredients

Lamb – keep it local if you can. I use lamb steak (no bones) or hotpot chops, but some swear by neck. Ask your butcher for advice

A little seasoned flour – toss the prepared meat in it to thicken the gravy

2 large onions, peeled and reasonably finely chopped

4 or 5 large white potatoes, peeled and sliced into rounds about 5mm thick

Thyme – fresh or dried

3 or 4 carrots, peeled and chopped into chunky slices (optional)

Lamb stock (a cube or powder is fine)

Salt and pepper

Method

Slow Cooker Method

1   In a large frying pan, gently fry off your lamb and vegetables to brown them slightly. Do this in batches if the pan is not big enough.

2   Set your slow cooker to low. Layer the lamb, vegetable, thyme and potatoes until all the ingredients are in the pot. Add stock until it just covers the top layer.

3   Cook on high for 6 to 10 hours. Test for seasoning

4   If you would like a crispy top, for the final 30 minutes of cooking place the hotpot in an oven-proof cooking dish and bake until crispy.

Conventional Oven

5   Pre-heat your oven to 150C/gas 2. In a large frying pan, gently fry off your lamb and vegetables to brown them slightly. Do this in batches if the pan is not big enough.

6   Layer your meat and vegetables with the thyme in your oven-proof casserole dish. Top with a final layer of potatoes. Add stock until it just covers the top layer.

7   Cover and bake for approximately 3 hours. When the lamb is meltingly tender and the vegetables are soft, remove the lid and bake for another 30 minutes or so until the top is crispy and golden.

8   Lancashire hotpot is traditionally served with pickled red cabbage, pickled beetroot or pickled onions.

Butter Pie

On my food blog this recipe is the most popular by far. For those of you who haven't experienced this delightful traditional Lancashire delicacy, butter pie is a shortcrust pastry case filled with potato, onion and butter. Its origins are vague, but it is thought to have been created by Roman Catholic workers as a filling wholesome meal for Friday, when devout Catholics do not eat meat. Hence it's other local names, Friday pie or Catholic pie.

Ingredients

Shortcrust pastry (out of a packet is fine, or you could make your own)

1 large onion, thinly sliced

3 large white potatoes, peeled and thinly sliced

Salt and pepper

Butter

A little milk or beaten egg

Method

1   Pre heat the oven to 180C/gas 4.

2   First, parboil your potato and onion in water or very weak vegetable stock until the vegetables are just softened but still retain their shape.

3   Line a large pie tin with pastry, and then roll out the remaining pastry to make the lid of the pie.

4   Layer the drained cooked potato and onion into the dish, adding dots of butter and a little salt and pepper to each layer until you have filled the pie dish.

5   Top the pie with the pastry lid. Trim off the excess pastry and seal and crimp the edges. Brush with a little beaten egg or milk.

6   Bake for 30 to 40 minutes until golden brown. Serve hot with green vegetables, mushy peas and brown or red sauce.

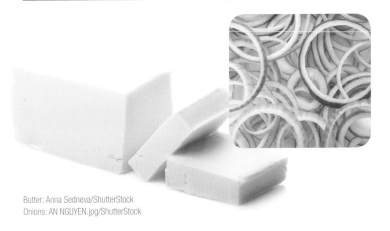

Butter: Anna Sedneva/ShutterStock
Onions: AN NGUYEN.jpg/ShutterStock

Lancashire Chees
and Courgette Ba

Another great recipe featuring Lancashire cheese – a very versatile ingredient and a fabulous cooking cheese, combined here with the vegetable I have a love hate-relationship with – the courgette. This is a dish created to use up more of my home-grown courgette crop. It makes an economical lunch dish for two greedy people, or four if served with a salad or side vegetable.

Ingredients

1 large white onion, chopped finely

Large knob of butter

Fresh rosemary, pulled into sprigs and finely chopped

300g baby new potatoes, chopped into large cubes

2 large courgettes, chopped into large cubes

150ml quality vegetable stock
(you could make your own, but a cube or powder is fine)

100g Lancashire cheese

100g fresh white breadcrumbs (easily made in the food processor or blender)

e

ke

Method

1	Preheat your oven to 180C/gas 4.
2	Start by sweating off the onion in the butter to soften it without colouring.
3	Add about 1 tbsp of the chopped rosemary and the potatoes to the pan. Stir, and then cover the pan and cook gently for about 10 minutes. Watch the potatoes for sticking; stir every 3 to 4 minutes.
4	Add the courgettes to the pan, stir and then add the stock. Put the lid on the pan and bring to a simmer.
3	For the topping, mix the breadcrumbs, a tablespoon of chopped rosemary and approx 50 g of grated Lancashire cheese.
6	Remove the pan from the heat, pour into your casserole dish, crumble the remaining 50 g of Lancashire cheese onto the potato, onion and courgette mixture and then top with the breadcrumb mixture.
7	Bake for approximately 30 to 45 minutes until golden and most of the moisture has evaporated. Serve immediately.

Paul Koornen/Shutterstock

unverdorben jr/Shutterstock

Lancashire Parkin

A traditional bonfire treat around these parts, and very different to the Yorkshire version. This is a great warmer and fairly healthy given the amount of oatmeal in the mixture. Ideally you should let this sit in an airtight tin for at least three or four days after baking for it to be at its best.

Ingredients

225g fine oatmeal

225g self-raising flour

225g soft brown sugar

Pinch of sea salt

1 ½ dsp ground ginger

225g margarine or butter

125g treacle

125g golden syrup

1 egg

Method

1	Pre-heat your oven to 170C/gas 3. Oil and line a large square tin.
2	Place the oatmeal, flour, sugar, salt and ginger in a bowl. Rub in the margarine or butter until you have a texture like fine breadcrumbs.
3	Add the treacle and syrup and the beaten egg. Mix thoroughly and pour into the lined tin.
4	Bake for 1 to 1 ½ hours, or until a skewer comes out clean. Cover with foil if the top is colouring too quickly.
5	Allow to cool in the tin. Store wrapped in baking parchment or aluminium foil for a few days. Serve cut in to chunky squares.

Monkey Business Images/Shutterstock

Tea Loaf

I love this tea loaf recipe because it's made all in one pan, so if you
hate washing up this is the recipe for you. The resultant cake is moist,
flavourful and very comforting, just the thing to have stored in a tin for
a treat after a wet and windy walk in the countryside. You can ring the
changes by using more unusual varieties of tea, such as rooibosch,
Earl Grey or chai, in the mixture.

Ingredients

120g salted butter
....
1 cup of strongly brewed tea
....
225g mixed dried fruit
....
1 tsp bicarbonate of soda
....
1 tsp mixed spice
....
225g self-raising flour
....
120g granulated sugar
....
1 egg
....

Method

1	Pre-heat the oven to 180C/gas 4. Grease and line a loaf tin.
2	Take a large pan and melt the butter over a low heat. Add the dried fruit and the cup of tea to the pan, bring to the boil and simmer for 2 minutes (this plumps the fruit up).
3	Remove from the heat and allow to cool for 5 minutes or so. Now add all the other ingredients, mixing well and working quickly.
4	Once thoroughly mixed, scrape into your prepared tin and level the top. Bake for about 45 minutes to an hour, until a skewer comes out clean.
5	Allow to cool in the tin for about 10 minutes, and then turn out onto a wire rack to cool fully. Stores well wrapped in foil.

MShev/Shutterstock

Goosnargh Cakes

Goosnargh, for those not in the know, is a village just outside Preston in Lancashire. The cakes that bear the village's name are in fact more like shortbread biscuits, featuring the underrated spice caraway in a thick buttery base. Also affectionately known as seed cakes, these are a great bake for a traditional afternoon tea table.

Ingredients

170g plain flour

85g butter

60g caster sugar

1 dsp caraway seeds

Method

1   Pre-heat the oven to 160C/gas 3. Sieve the plain flour and sugar into a large bowl. Rub in the butter to make a fine crumb. Add the caraway seeds to the mixture and mix well.

2   Now start to form a dough by squeezing the mixture together. Add a tiny drop of water if you need to.

3   Tip your dough onto a floured surface and gently roll out to 5mm thickness. Cut small rounds using a biscuit cutter of your desired size.

4   Place on a greased baking sheet. Bake until firm, but with no noticeable colour. Dust with a little caster sugar and allow to fully cool on the tray.

Vova Shevchuk/Shutterstock

Chorley Cakes

Personally I love Chorley cakes, and even shop-bought ones are pretty good in my opinion. They are much nicer than their relative the Eccles cake; for me they must be served spread generously with butter, but some people prefer them plain.

Chorley cakes are a buttery shortcrust pastry parcel filled with a juicy dried fruit filling, rather homely-looking but very tasty. Chorley cakes are often made with the off-cuts of pastry left over after making a pie.

Ingredients

1 packet of shortcrust pastry (thawed if frozen) or use homemade if you prefer

150g raisins, currants or sultanas, or a mixture

50g soft brown sugar

1/2 tsp ground mixed spice (optional)

25g butter (or small knob)

Flour for rolling out

Beaten egg or milk for glazing

Method

1	Preheat the oven to 180C/gas 4 and grease a couple of baking trays.
2	Roll out the pastry into a large round. Using a saucer as a template, cut out circles of pastry.
3	In a small bowl, mix the dried fruit, sugar, butter and spice into a chunky paste. Place a large dollop of the dried fruit mixture in the centre of each circle of pastry.
4	Fold the outside of the pastry over the filling. When it is covered, turn the parcel over and cut a couple of slits in the top and press down firmly to remove any air. You could use a rolling pin for this if you wish.
5	Once you have used up all the pastry, place the cakes on a baking tray and brush the tops with a little beaten egg or milk. Bake until firm; the pastry should be cooked and the tops should be lightly golden.
6	Cool on a wire rack. Serve plain or slathered with butter.

Monkey Business Images/
Shutterstock

A deep-dish pie filled with delicious apples and creamy Lancashire cheese. This can be served as an elegant dessert, but it also makes a super tea time treat.

Ingredients

1 packet of ready-made shortcrust pastry, or make your own

900g cooking apples, peeled, cored and cut into chunks

½ tsp ground cinnamon

75g sultanas

5 tbsp maple syrup

150g Lancashire cheese, crumbled

1 medium egg, beaten

Method

1   Preheat the oven to 200C/gas 6.

2   Roll out the pastry on a lightly floured surface and use to line a deep 20cm pie dish or loose-bottomed flan tin. Prick the bottom and chill whilst preparing the filling. Reserve the pastry trimmings to decorate the top of the pie.

3   Place the apples, cinnamon, sultanas and maple syrup in a pan. Cover and cook over a gentle heat until the apples just begin to soften. Remove from the heat and fold in the crumbled Lancashire cheese.

4   Spoon into the pastry case. Re-roll the pastry trimmings and cut into strips about 1cm wide. Make a lattice pattern on top of the pie and brush with beaten egg to glaze.

5   Bake for 30 to 35 minutes until the pastry is golden and crisp.

margouillat photo/Shutterstock

The combination of fruitcake and cheese is a tradition in many households in the north of England, and it works particularly well with creamy Lancashire cheese. However, you could also substitute a tangy mature Cheddar or a mild Wensleydale if you prefer.

Ingredients

500g plain flour

4 tsp baking powder

2 tsp mixed spice

1 tsp ground cinnamon

200g soft dark brown sugar

450g mixed dried fruit (raisins, sultanas, cherries, figs – whatever you have to hand)

200g unsalted butter, softened, plus extra for spreading

4 eggs

2 to **3 tbsp** milk (you may not need all of it)

Lancashire cheese, sliced, to serve

Method

1   Preheat the oven to 160C/gas 2. Grease and line a 20cm square cake tin.

2   Mix the flour, baking powder, mixed spice, cinnamon, brown sugar and dried fruit together in a bowl until well combined. Add the butter and crack in the eggs. Mix well, and then add just enough milk to give a smooth batter. Pour the batter into the prepared cake tin.

3   Bake in the oven for one and three-quarters to two hours, or until the cake is golden-brown and springy to the touch and a skewer comes out clean. Remove from the oven and set aside to cool.

4   To serve, thickly slice the cake and spread each slice with butter. Fry in a hot pan for one minute on both sides, or until golden-brown all over. Serve each cake slice with a slice of cheese.

Verkhovynets Taras/Shutterstock

Lancashire Chees
and Mushroom Ra

A quick snack dish, great to serve for a quick lunch or an impromptu supper. The secret is the Lancashire cheese; make sure you get hold of a creamy or a tasty Lancashire, because crumbly just won't do here. A true Lancashire cheese should made in Lancashire from local milk; most of the genuine producers are based in the Garstang area, near Preston.

Ingredients

Quality white bread for your toast – ideally a sourdough, or perhaps the soda bread from earlier in this book

Lancashire cheese – creamy or tasty, so that it melts well

Mushrooms (or you could use onions)

Freshly ground pepper

Brown sauce or a chutney (optional)

ebit

Method

1	In a frying pan, cook your mushrooms or onion until soft.
2	Add the cheese to the same pan and melt gently. Add your sauce or chutney if you are using them. Meanwhile, toast your bread.
3	Once your bread is toasted and the cheese melted, it's an easy assembly job to top the toast with the melted cheese mixture.
4	Pop under a preheated grill for a few minutes until the topping is bubbly. Devour immediately.

JIANG HONGYAN/Shutterstock

Brown Shrimp-Top

The north-west of England, particularly the areas of Morecambe Bay and Southport, are justifiably famous for the tiny brown shrimps found in the Ribble and Lune estuaries. They are caught, cooked and potted locally into tiny pots with flavoured spiced butter. These delights are available to buy in most supermarkets. Ask if you can't find them, because they make a great easy starter for a dinner party or a decadent snack.

Ingredients

1 pot of brown shrimp for 2 people (or 1 greedy person)

1 English muffin – serves 2

Salad leaves (ideally watercress or rocket)

ped Muffin

Method

1   Spilt your English muffin and toast until lightly golden.

2   Heat a small frying pan over a gentle heat. Empty the contents of your shrimp pot into your pan. Heat gently until the butter is melted and the shrimp warmed through.

3   Put half of your toasted muffin on a serving plate and spoon on the warmed shrimps and the melted spiced butter. Arrange your salad leaves alongside the topped muffin.

4   Serve and wait for the praise. If you are feeling especially extravagant you could top the shrimp with a soft poached egg.

Subbotina Anna/Shutterstock

Tomato Tart

A favourite in our household, this tart is a great and fairly impressive supper dish to serve in the summertime with a green salad and a chilled white wine. The dish is even better if you can use home-grown tomatoes; it seems to capture the scent of summer. If you aren't growing your own tomatoes, try to buy locally-grown cherry or baby plum tomatoes to avoid a watery tasteless dish. I nearly always use ready-made flaky pastry, but shortcrust works fine too.

Ingredients

1 packet of ready-made flaky pastry (if frozen thawed)

1 kg of fresh ripe tomatoes, sliced thinly

½ jar of pesto sauce, caramelised onion chutney or similar (optional)

Polenta/cornmeal

Salt and pepper

Caster sugar

Method

1   Pre-heat your oven according to the instructions on your pastry pack.

2   Roll out your pastry to the size of your baking tray. Pinch or fold all round the outer edge to form a crust to contain your filling.

3   If you are using pesto or chutney, smear this across base. If you are not using pesto or chutney, sprinkle the base with polenta to create a crispy bottom for the tomatoes.

4   Cover the base with overlapping slices of tomato. Sprinkle with a little pepper and caster sugar (this is to ensure your tomatoes are sweet and flavourful). Do not use salt, as it will draw the moisture from the tomatoes and create a soggy bottom.

5   Bake in the oven until well risen and golden and the tomatoes have started to caramelise. Allow to cool slightly before serving; it's also great cold.

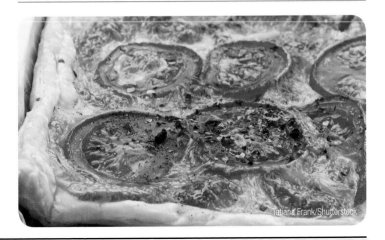

Tatiana Frank/Shutterstock

Black Pudding and

Combining two great northern ingredients, this is a great supper dish or a canapé if you are entertaining. It sounds unusual, but it works and it is very easy to pull together. I have also served this to so-called black pudding haters and have managed to convert them to black pudding lovers.

Ingredients

8 slices of black pudding

200g fresh rhubarb, washed and chopped into chunks

16 sheets filo pastry (ready-made), thawed if frozen

1 white onion, peeled and chopped finely

100ml dry cider (local if you can get it)

Freshly ground black pepper

Freshly ground nutmeg

Olive oil or vegetable oil

Rhubarb Parcels

Method

1   Pre-heat the oven to 160C/gas 2.

2   Fry the black pudding slices in a little olive oil. Remove from the pan to a plate when they start to colour.

3   In the same pan, cook the onion until softened. Now add the rhubarb chunks and cider, and simmer until the rhubarb starts to disintegrate. Taste and season with pepper and nutmeg. Remove from heat.

4   To make the parcels, use 1 sheet of filo folded in half. Place a dessert spoon of rhubarb mixture in the centre and top with half a slice of black pudding. Fold in the corners to create a "money bag" parcel.

5   Place carefully on a baking tray and bake for around 20 to 30 minutes until the pastry is cooked and golden. Serve hot or chilled.

Edward Westmacott/Shutterstock

Pabkov/Shutterstock

Formby Asparagus a

English asparagus is, in my humble opinion, the King of vegetables. Lancashire is very fortunate to have on its doorstep an area where this vegetable can be grown, with the ideal conditions of sandy soil and just the right amount of sunshine. That place is Formby, although it is probably more famous for the art installation Another Place by Antony Gormley than it is for its asparagus.

Search out local asparagus if at all possible and use it while it is in season. This is a great supper dish, and I am sure it is one you will make over and over again.

Ingredients

Bundle of fresh local asparagus, bottom trimmed

Really fresh eggs, one per person

A couple of drops of cider vinegar

Salt and pepper

Bread to serve (optional)

Method

1	Steam your asparagus.
2	Poach your eggs in a pan with gently simmering water which has had a couple of drops of cider vinegar added. I cook mine for about 2 minutes until the white is firmed and is opaque, but the yolk is still soft and runny.
3	Drain the eggs onto kitchen paper. Serve the asparagus topped with the poached egg, sprinkled with a little seasoning.

Fotogroove/Shutterstock

Shepherd's Pie

Cottage pie (made with beef) or Shepherd's pie (made with lamb) are the kings of comfort food, can be made a day in advance (tastes even better) and represents great value for money! I like to sprinkle a handful of strong cheese on top.

Ingredients SERVES 4

Vegetable oil

100g lean lamb mince

1 large onion, finely chopped

1 carrot, finely chopped

2 celery sticks, finely chopped

Clove garlic, finely chopped

6 mushrooms, sliced

1 sprig thyme

200ml stock (Marigold is the best, but any good stock cube will do)

Worcestershire sauce

1 tin chopped tomatoes

450g potatoes

Knob of butter

Salt

Freshly ground black pepper

Handful of grated or crumbled cheese

Method

1 Heat a tablespoon of oil in a large pan and gently brown the mince. Remove and add the chopped vegetables to the pan. Cook for about five minutes or until they've softened a bit.

2 Add the mince, a good dash of relish, the tomatoes, stock, thyme and season generously with salt & pepper. Let it bubble away for about an hour, until the stock has reduced by half.

3 In the meantime, peel the potatoes, cut them into small-ish chunks, put in cold water with a pinch of salt and bring to the boil. Let them simmer away for about 20 minutes, until they're soft.

4 Drain, add a knob of butter, a splash of milk, and mash. Put the mince mixture into an ovenproof dish, cover with the mashed potatoes, sprinkled on the cheese and put in a medium hot oven for about 15 minutes until the cheese has browned up. Serve with minted peas and pickled red cabbage.

violeta pasat/Shutterstock

Store Cupboard Staples

Atora suet

Baking powder

Balsamic vinegar

Bay leaves

Bay leaves

Bicarbonate of soda

Black peppercorns

Block of parmesan

Chilli flakes

Cider vinegar

Currants

Dried thyme

English mustard

Fast-action yeast

Glace cherries

Golden syrup

Gourmet Garden Herbs & Spices (ginger, garlic, coriander, basil, chilli, thai spices)

Ground cinnamon

Ground ginger

Harissa

Jar of black olives

Kallo stock cubes

Lemon juice squeezy

Lincolnshire Honey

Malt vinegar

Marigold Swiss Vegetable Bouillon

Olive oil

Rape seed oil

Ready made short crust pastry

Red wine vinegar

Sea salt

(Maldon is the best, but any will do)

Strong white bread flour

Sultanas

Sunflower oil

Tinned butter beans

Tinned chopped tomatoes

Tinned red kidney beans

Tomato passata

White wine vinegar

Whole nutmeg

Wholegrain mustard

Wholemeal flour

Worcestershire Sauce

About
Linzi Barrow

Linzi Barrow is passionate creative home cook and baker with a love of local, seasonal food. She lives in Lancashire with her husband Ian, two house cats and three chickens, Linzi is a food writer and blogger and blogs personally at the popular food blog and has also had recipes featured in various local and national magazines and in several cookery books over the years. She is a regular contributor to local radio and has also done some television work.
Linzi's blog can be found at Lancashire-food. blogspot.co.uk